Johnnie Carr

Johnnie

The Life of
Johnnie Rebecca Carr

With Her Friends Rosa Parks,
E. D. Nixon, Martin Luther King, Jr.,
and Others in the Civil Rights Struggle

as told to Randall Williams

with illustrations by Jeffrey Hurst

NewSouth Books
Montgomery | Louisville

NewSouth Books
P.O. Box 1588
Montgomery, AL 36102

www.newsouthbooks.com

ISBN-13: 978-1-60306-033-2
ISBN-10: 1-60306-033-2

Design by Randall Williams
Printed in the U.S.A.

For Our Families

Chores on the Daniels farm

When she was a little girl, Johnnie Rebecca Daniels lived on a farm outside Montgomery, Alabama. She would grow up to become a leader of the African Americans in Montgomery as they fought against segregation and discrimination. But her childhood was spent on the wonderful farm, with chickens, cows, horses, mules, pigs, dogs, and cats.

Her daddy, John Daniels, and her mama, Anna Richmond Daniels, were farmers. They raised corn, peas, tomatoes, okra, potatoes, turnips, collards, butterbeans, squash, and all the other good vegetables that grew so well in the soft, rich dirt of the Daniels farm.

When the vegetables were ready for harvesting, Johnnie would help her mother preserve some of them for the winter months. This was hot work, because all the cooking and canning was done on a big black wood-burning stove. Johnnie was born in 1911, and it would be many years before country people had electric or gas stoves. In fact, the Daniels farm did not even have indoor plumbing. To get water, you had to work the handle on a pump near the barn, and then carry the water in a bucket to the house. Life on a farm was hard work.

The Daniels farm also had lots of fruit trees: peach, plum, grapes, scuppernongs, pears, and

Feeding corn
to the chickens

apples. Milk and butter came from the family's cow. Eggs and fresh meat came from the Rhode Island Red and White Leghorn chickens—Mrs. Daniels was very proud of her chickens. And there was plenty of bacon, ham, pork chops, ribs, and sausage from the hogs the family raised. Mr. Daniels even kept a dozen or more hives of bees which he would rob to get honey for cooking and for the table.

Johnnie liked to watch her father rob the bees. The hives were in the orchard, so the bees could get nectar from the blossoms of the fruit trees. To protect himself from bee stings, Mr. Daniels would wear a long-sleeved shirt and gloves. And he would put a veil over his hat to protect his face and neck. Then he would light a fire of leaves and moss inside a special blower. He would direct the smoke into the hives, which would make the bees drowsy and still. Then he could take out the combs, which would be dripping with thick, delicious honey.

Robbing the bees of their honey

"Johnnie," he would say, "would you like a
piece of honeycomb?"

Naturally, Johnnie was just dying to have a
piece of the sweet comb. Mr. Daniels would cut
off a little piece, and she would chew it up until
all the sweetness was gone. Then she would spit
out the waxy comb that was left. This was better
than candy, she thought.

When the bees woke up from their naps

caused by the smoke, they would be angry that they had been robbed. Johnnie knew that it was a good idea to stay out of the orchard while the bees were angry. But soon the bees would settle down and then they would go back to work building new combs and making more honey.

This was a cycle of nature, and Johnnie, like all farm children, knew that life ran in cycles. Crops were planted, tended, and harvested. Eggs became chickens, and chickens laid more eggs. A squealing little pig grew up to become a big sow with a dozen squealing pigs of her own. And some pigs grew up to become hams and pork chops.

Johnnie's mama and daddy taught her to respect life, and to love growing things. They taught her that although life could be difficult at times, God's mercy was bountiful for those who worked hard. Johnnie never forgot these lessons.

Mrs. Daniels had a large pantry where she

kept the canned vegetables and the jars of jelly. Johnnie liked to watch her mother line up the vegetables in rows in the pantry. The jars of yellow squash, green beans, brown peas, purple grape jelly, amber apple jelly, and golden honey made beautiful patterns in the pantry. All of this food wouldn't be just for the Daniels family. Mrs. Daniels would give food to other families that did not have enough. This was another lesson that Johnnie never forgot.

Almost everything the Daniels family needed, they could grow on their farm. To get money for other things, Mrs. Daniels loaded vegetables, eggs, butter, and milk on a wagon. Mr. Daniels hitched the horse to the wagon, and Mrs. Daniels drove into town, where she peddled the vegetables along the streets to the city housewives. Then she would have enough money to go to a store for flour, meal, sugar, shoes, cloth, and other necessities.

Mrs. Daniels was known in Montgomery as a

great baker of cakes. White women would drive their buggies or cars out to the Daniels farm to get cakes baked for them. Sometimes they would bring their children, and while the white women were in the house talking with Mrs. Daniels, Johnnie and the children would play in the yard.

After a while, Mrs. Daniels would call, "Johnnie! Bowl to lick!"

And Johnnie and the little white children would run to the kitchen to get the bowl that

Licking the bowl

Mrs. Daniels had mixed the cake batter in. All the children would lick out the delicious batter.

In those days, in Alabama and other parts of the South, blacks and whites were segregated, or separated, from each other by law and custom. They did not go to school together, or to church together. But on these cake-baking afternoons when she was a little girl, segregation was unknown to Johnnie. In her later life, she would remember those times when she played with white children and when white women sat visiting with her mother in the kitchen while cakes were baking in the great black wood-burning stove.

Johnnie was the baby of the family. She had five older brothers and a sister, but, as the youngest, she was her daddy's favorite. He liked for Johnnie to go with him when he had business in town. He would hitch the buggy, then he would say, "Come on, Johnnie. Let's go."

When the watermelons got ripe, he would pick

the largest one for her. "Johnnie, this is your watermelon," he would say, with a wink. Sometimes her older sister would be jealous.

When she was nine, Johnnie's beloved father caught pneumonia and died. Johnnie cried and cried. She missed her father, and she could not understand why God would take her daddy from her. But Mrs. Daniels gathered the family together. They prayed, and they mourned their loss. In time, Johnnie got over the hurt, but she always remembered her father.

After Mr. Daniels died, it was hard for Mrs. Daniels to manage the farm by herself. Some of the older children were grown by now and had moved into their own homes. So Mrs. Daniels moved herself and the younger children into town.

Johnnie then began going to a new school, the Montgomery Industrial School. This was a famous school for African American girls. It was often called Miss White's School, because the principal was a spinster named Alice White, a white woman who had come from the North to help educate Negro girls in the South. Miss White believed not only in teaching the "Three R's" but she also taught cooking, sewing, and other occupational courses. The education at Miss White's School was considered to be far superior to that at the limited public schools then available in Montgomery for black children.

It was at Miss White's School that Johnnie Daniels met and became friends with Rosa Louise McCauley. When Rosa grew up, she married Raymond A. Parks, and as Mrs. Rosa Parks, she became famous when she resisted segregation on a Montgomery city bus in 1955.

This incident led to the Montgomery Bus Boycott and the Civil Rights Movement, in which the grown-up Rosa and Johnnie both played significant parts.

But at Miss White's School, they were simply schoolgirl friends.

Her children's education was very important to Mrs. Daniels. She had only been able to go through the third or fourth grade herself. She wanted to make sure her children had a better opportunity, so she worked hard and saved and sacrificed to pay the fees for Johnnie to attend Miss White's School and for Johnnie's brother, Alfred, to attend the Booker Washington Swane School.

By 1927, Miss White was getting old and in poor health, so she closed her school. Johnnie was in the seventh grade. In later years, she would go back to school to improve her education, but the closing of Miss White's School ended one chapter in Johnnie's life.

In those days, many young women and men, both black and white, married at early ages. Johnnie was sixteen. She knew that her mother had a hard time supporting her family on the small wages she earned doing cooking and cleaning in the homes of white Montgomerians.

So Johnnie, at age sixteen, made up her mind to marry Jack Jordan, a young man she had met. She did not tell her mother of her plans. One day she and Jack went to a preacher's home and were married. Johnnie became Mrs. Jack Jordan. Then they went home and told Mrs. Daniels.

Her mother was upset because Johnnie was her youngest child and because she knew how hard it was for a young couple with no money and limited education to make a decent living. But she dried her tears and welcomed the newlyweds into her home.

At age sixteen, Johnnie Jordan began learning how to be a wife. For the first year, she and Jack lived with his grandparents. Then the young couple rented a one-room house with an added-on kitchen and were truly on their own. In 1928, their first daughter, Annie Belle, was born.

Johnnie and Jack Jordan worked hard to support themselves and Annie Belle. But the 1930s were the years of the Great Depression, and jobs and money were scarce. Jack worked at Greenwood Cemetery and earned twelve dollars a week. Like her mother had done, Johnnie went to work as a domestic, cooking and cleaning in the homes of white people. She earned about three dollars a week.

In 1932, Johnnie gave birth to another daughter, Alma. With two children to raise, Johnnie could not work outside the home, and times became even harder for the Jordan family.

Johnnie knew that she and Jack would never really be able to progress unless they improved their education. So after the children were a little older, Johnnie went back to school. But Jack would not go. He decided that he had enough education. He also began to drink and to gamble. This made Johnnie unhappy and very sad.

One day, she went to town with her husband, and she learned that he had spent their rent money to pay a gambling debt. She left him in town

Praying for guidance

and went home alone to their house.

She fell on her knees and prayed to God for guidance. She prayed for a long time, and when she had finished she had made up her mind that she and Jack could not remain together. She was determined to improve her education and make a better life for their daughters. But he was content with things as they were.

So Jack and Johnnie Jordan separated, and she became a single mother to their two children. By this time, Johnnie's mother, Mrs. Daniels, was old, and she was living with Johnnie, Annie Belle, and Alma.

While Johnnie worked and went to school, Mrs. Daniels would look after the children. Johnnie finished junior high school and began on her high school classes.

But, because she needed money, she decided to change course and get training that would provide her with a better job. So she took a course in practical nursing, and then she was able to get work looking after sick people in their homes.

Often, she sat up with sick people at night, napping herself whenever she could. This sched-

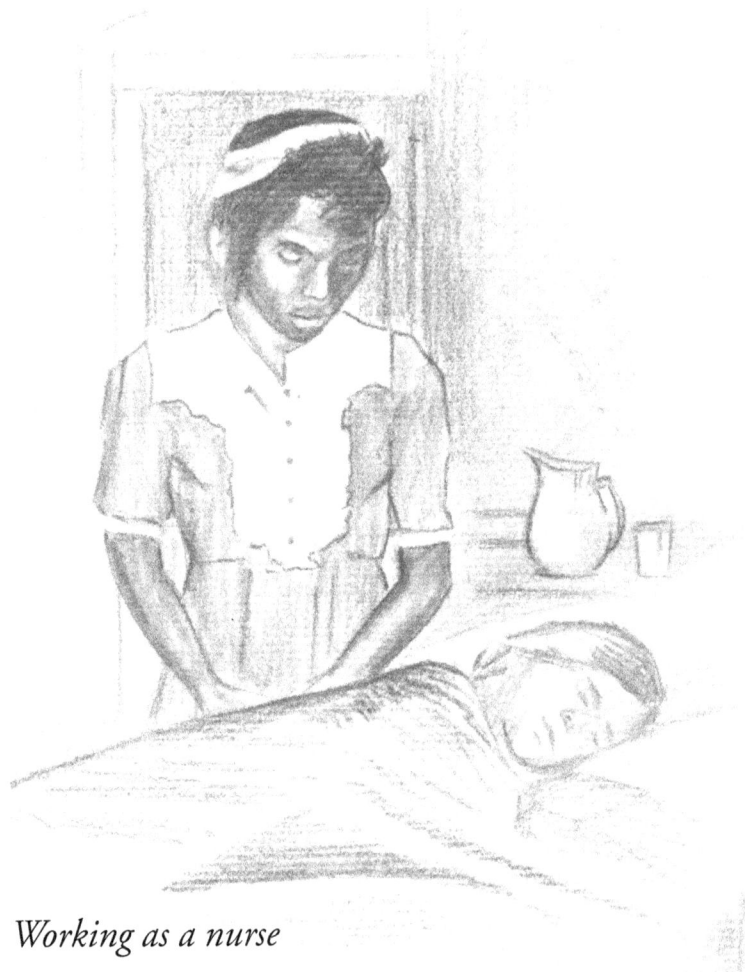

Working as a nurse

ule allowed her to be at home with her children during the day.

In time, Mrs. Johnnie Jordan became known in the community, as her mother had been before her, as a person who was active in her church and could be counted on to help those who were less fortunate. She had made three dollars a week as a maid, but she made fifteen dollars a week as a practical nurse. She was careful to put aside a little money each time she was paid, and gradually life improved for her and her daughters.

One day at church, another member of the congregation, a Mr. Z. H. Wilson, asked if she would be interested in selling insurance. "Mrs. Jordan," he said to her, "I've noticed that you meet people well and have a good way with them. I believe you might like a job selling insurance."

At first, she thought little of this suggestion. But Mr. Wilson kept after her, until finally she said she would give the insurance field a try.

She discovered that she did like traveling around Montgomery, meeting new people, and selling them insurance policies.

Her new job gave her more opportunities to become involved in the community, and she joined some clubs and other groups.

One of the organizations she joined was the National Association for the Advancement of Colored People—which was known as the NAACP. Founded in 1905 by both blacks and whites, the NAACP worked in Alabama and other states to try to improve conditions for African Americans.

The leader of the NAACP in Montgomery was E. D. Nixon. Mr. Nixon was a big man with a booming voice and a fearless manner. He made his living as a porter in the Pullman cars on the railroad, and he was friends with the great African American labor leader, A. Philip Randolph.

Mr. Nixon and Mrs. Johnnie Jordan became friends and worked together to improve conditions in Montgomery. Segregation was a way of life throughout the South. Slavery had ended after the Civil War, but slavery had been replaced by the rigid system of segregation. African Americans could not eat in the same restaurants, sleep in the same hotels, use the same public restrooms, or even drink from the same public water fountains as whites. African Americans were the last to get good jobs, and were usually paid less than whites for the same jobs. Many jobs were simply not available to African Americans.

The social customs of the day were also disrespectful to African Americans. All white people were called Mr. or Mrs. or Miss, but black people were called only by their first names. Even an illiterate white person would call the most distinguished black teacher or doctor by his first name. Certainly not all white people were disrespectful, but the segregated system usually led to very unfair treatment of black citizens.

African Americans who visited the homes of whites had to go in and out of the back door. There were also "colored" entrances to movie theaters and "colored" waiting rooms in bus stations, doctors' offices, and other public places.

These segregation customs were deeply resented by African Americans, and they were a symbol of other discrimination by police, government, banks, and virtually every aspect of life in Montgomery and other places in the South.

One day Mrs. Jordan's name was in the newspaper in connection with an NAACP activity. Her childhood friend, Rosa McCauley—now Mrs. Raymond Parks—saw the article and got in touch with her. Mrs. Parks also joined the NAACP, and Mrs. Jordan and Mrs. Parks renewed their friendship and worked together with Mr. Nixon and other African American community leaders.

Gradually, small changes began to occur. After World War II, large numbers of black servicemen returned home after helping defeat the forces of tyranny and racism in Europe and the Pacific. These men were determined that they would not be denied democracy at home after having fought for democracy abroad.

More and more African Americans began to register to vote. And protests began to be made against segregated schools and discrimination in jobs and other areas. In parts of the country outside the segregated South, some whites began to join with African Americans in battling segregation laws. Lawyers for the NAACP began filing lawsuits, and small victories began to be won.

There was a new feeling of optimism among African Americans that change might finally be coming to places like Montgomery.

Of course, Johnnie Jordan, Mr. Nixon, and Mrs. Parks, along with other leaders, knew that changes would be won slowly and only after hard battles.

During this time, something wonderful was happening in Johnnie Jordan's personal life, too. After divorcing Jack Jordan, she had just about given up on men. But one day, she noticed a quiet, polite, handsome young insurance agent who worked for another company. Gradually, she and Arlam Carr fell in love, and on February 12, 1944, they married.

Now she was Mrs. Arlam Carr, and she was very happy. Arlam and Johnnie Carr both believed in their jobs, their church, and their community. They loved each other very much, and she again had a happy home.

When she and Mr. Carr married, Annie Belle was sixteen and Alma was twelve. Before long, they were grown and had begun families of their own. Mrs. Carr was already a grandmother when the next miracle happened in her life—she became pregnant again.

Eighteen years after Alma was born, Mrs. Carr gave birth to Arlam Jr.

So, the years passed and Arlam and Johnnie Carr sold insurance, raised their family, and worked in their church and community.

On the night of December 1, 1955, Mrs. Carr was getting ready to go to bed when her phone rang. Mr. Nixon was on the line.

"Mrs. Carr," he said.

"Yeah," said Mrs. Carr.

"Well, they put the wrong person in jail," Mr. Nixon said.

"Who they put in jail?" said Mrs. Carr.

"They arrested Rosa Parks," replied Mr. Nixon.

"You don't mean to tell me that they arrested Rosa Parks?" said Mrs. Carr.

"Yes," said Mr. Nixon. "They arrested Rosa Parks on the bus today. They put the wrong person in jail."

That was how Mrs. Carr found out that her friend, Rosa Parks, had been arrested earlier that day in downtown Montgomery. When he called Mrs. Carr, Mr. Nixon had just returned home from the Montgomery City Jail, where he had gone with his white friends, attorney and Mrs.

Clifford Durr, to arrange bail for Mrs. Parks. Clifford and Virginia Durr were white, but they were friends of Mr. Nixon, Mrs. Parks, and Mrs. Carr.

When Mr. Nixon had first heard the news that Mrs. Parks was arrested, he called the Montgomery jail to find out about the charges. The jailers told Mr. Nixon that it was none of his business. So Mr. Nixon called Mr. Durr, who called the jail himself. As a white man and a lawyer, he was able to get the information that the jailers would not give to Mr. Nixon, and then he and Mrs. Durr volunteered to go downtown with Mr. Nixon to the jail.

Being a lawyer, Mr. Durr could help Mr. Nixon with the procedures to post a bond for the release of Mrs. Parks. But, although Mr. Durr was a Montgomery native, he and his family had only recently returned to Alabama after living for many years in Washington, D.C. The Durrs had not yet bought property in Montgomery, so they could not post the bond for Mrs. Parks themselves. Mr. Nixon, however, was a property owner. He pledged his home as security for Mrs. Parks's bail, and then she was released from police custody.

Mr. Nixon explained to Mrs. Carr what had happened.

Around 6 p.m., Mrs. Parks had left her job at the Montgomery Fair department store and had boarded the Cleveland Avenue bus to go home. The buses were segregated. By law, whites boarded and sat at the front, and blacks boarded and sat at the rear of the bus. If there were not enough seats in the front for whites, then the driver would order black passengers to stand so the whites could sit down. This was another example of the humiliation that African Americans suffered under segregation.

When Mrs. Parks boarded the bus, there were four empty seats right behind the white section. She and three other black passengers sat down on that row. At the next stop, several white passengers got on the bus, but there were no more seats in the white section.

So the driver, Mr. J. F. Blake, told Mrs. Parks and the other three blacks seated on the row with her to move further toward the back of the bus. The other three black passengers moved, but Mrs. Parks did not.

Mrs. Parks said later that she did not get up because she was tired. And she was. She was tired of segregation laws. Tired of African Americans being mistreated because of their color. Tired of discrimination and oppression and worse. When she refused to move, the bus driver called the police, and Mrs. Rosa Parks—a quiet, dignified lady who had the respect of all who knew her—was arrested and charged with disorderly conduct.

Her arrest sent shock waves through the Montgomery African American community. This was not the first time a black bus passenger had been arrested for refusing to go along with segregated seating, but because of who she was, Mrs. Parks's arrest was immediately recognized as a good opportunity to challenge segregation.

Community leaders immediately set to work. While attorney Fred Gray prepared to defend Mrs. Parks in court, other leaders called meetings. The decision was quickly made for a one-day boycott of the buses on Monday, December 5, 1955, the day Mrs. Parks was to appear in court.

Professor Jo Ann Robinson of Alabama State University, and other members of a local organization named the Women's Political Council, wrote, printed, and distributed a flyer urging black Montgomerians to stay off the buses for that day as a protest against segregation.

Mr. E. D. Nixon even told a white newspaper reporter about the plans for the boycott. The reporter printed this story in the Sunday newspaper so that whites would know what the African

Americans "were up to," but his story also spread the word even more within the black community. All over town, black ministers preached sermons urging their congregations to boycott the buses the next day.

Among these ministers was the Rev. Dr. Martin Luther King, Jr., the pastor of the Dexter Avenue Baptist Church. Dr. King had only been in Montgomery for about a year, and he was only twenty-six years old. Most white citizens and many black citizens of Montgomery had never even heard of him.

But Dr. King commanded much respect in the black community, because he was the son of a well-known Atlanta preacher, and because he was well-educated—he was referred to as Dr. King because he had earned a doctoral degree from the theology school at Boston University. He was already recognized as an outstanding orator and a person who was wise and mature far beyond his years.

Mr. Nixon and Dr. King plan strategy

In fact, he was so well-respected that when a group of Montgomery's African American leaders met on the day after Mrs. Parks was arrested to plan a response, they elected Dr. King as the leader of the boycott organization.

This group was called the Montgomery Improvement Association, or the MIA for short. In the years to come, Mrs. Carr would become the president of the MIA, but Dr. King was the first president.

On Monday morning, December 5, 1955, Dr. King, his friend and fellow boycott leader Rev. Ralph Abernathy, Professor Jo Ann Robinson, Mr. E. D. Nixon, and other leaders got up early to see whether the boycott would work.

Because about 65 percent of the regular riders on the Montgomery City Lines buses were black, a successful boycott would be a powerful demonstration of how angry African Amerians were at being treated as second-class citizens.

Throughout the city of Montgomery that morning, the buses were virtually empty of black riders. The boycott was working.

Then a large group of Mrs. Parks's friends and supporters accompanied her to the Montgomery city court for her trial on the charge of violating the segregation ordinance. After a short hearing before Judge John Scott, she was found guilty and fined ten dollars. Her attorney, Fred Gray, immediately filed a notice that the conviction would be appealed.

As they left City Hall, the boycott leaders spread the word that there would be a mass meeting at 7 p.m. that night at the Holt Street Baptist Church to decide what to do next.

By 5 p.m., the church was already full, and by the time the meeting was to start several thousand black citizens were gathered outside. Loudspeakers were set up so those outside could hear the meeting going on inside.

For many of those at the meeting, it was their first time to actually hear Dr. King in person. There was singing, and a number of leaders made speeches about the long years of indignity that African Americans had endured on the Montgomery buses. Then Dr. King spoke. He told the people that the time had come to protest against the injustices his people had borne for so long. He began to teach about how love and non-violence could be used as weapons against bigotry and violence. He urged the people to join together and stand up for right and righteousness.

As Dr. King talked, those inside and outside the church were moved not only by his message, but by the power and conviction of how he spoke the message. In the years to come, people around the world would marvel at the strength of his voice and the eloquence with which he expressed his all-embracing philosophy of brotherhood, non-violence, and reconciliation. That night in the Holt Street Baptist Church was the first time he used these God-given talents to unite people toward such a goal.

Then he asked for a vote on whether the boycott should continue until the segregated bus seating policy was changed. The people inside the church, as well as those listening outside on the loudspeakers, responded with enthusiastic support for Mrs. Parks and for continuation of the boycott.

So, for the next year, African Americans in Montgomery refused to ride the segregated buses. Attorney Gray, with the help of other lawyers, including Clifford Durr, appealed Mrs. Parks's case and filed still more legal challenges to segregation. At the same time, Dr. King and the boycott leaders worked hard to keep up the support of the black community for the boycott.

It was a great sacrifice for many people to stay off the buses. Most regular bus riders did not have cars. Those who did have cars often gave rides to those who did not. The boycott leaders also organized a car pool system. Still, many African Americans had to walk wherever they went. This sacrifice was willingly made as people decided it was better to walk in dignity than to ride in segregation.

As the boycott went on, newspaper and televi-

Dr. King holds a press conference about the boycott

sion reporters from around the world began to
pay attention.

Citizens in other cities sent messages of support and money to pay for station wagons to set
up an informal transportation system. As the
spokesman for the bus boycott, Dr. King began
to be invited to other cities to give speeches about
the stand being made in Montgomery.

One story Dr. King liked to tell during his
speeches was of an elderly woman who was walk-

ing to her destination in Montgomery. Dr. King said he suggested that she go ahead and ride the bus since she was so old it might be too tiring for her to walk.

"Oh, no," she told him. "My feets is tired, but my soul is rested."

So, the black citizens of Montgomery continued to stay off the buses. Arlam and Johnnie Carr, like thousands of others, helped in the boycott in any way they could. They attended the weekly mass meetings that were being held in various churches each Monday night. These meetings were important to keep up the spirits of the community and to share information about the various court cases and the local responses to the boycott.

As time went by, the white Montgomery officials not only refused to negotiate the bus seating policies, but they arrested ninety-eight black leaders, including Mrs. Parks and Dr.

King, on charges of leading an illegal boycott. Other African Americans lost their jobs when their white employers learned they supported the boycott. Others were refused bank loans.

A Mississippi organization called the White Citizens Council, which had formed in opposition to school integration, held a big rally in Montgomery. Hundreds of whites became members of the group.

The Citizens Council claimed it was non-violent, but its members spoke angry words against the boycott and its leaders. This language made violent individuals and organizations like the Ku Klux Klan feel justified in taking stronger action.

During this time, a gang of white men kidnapped a black man, Willie Edwards, and forced him to jump off a Montgomery bridge. The victim could not swim and he drowned. Other black people were beaten by white hoodlums.

Bombs exploded at the home of Mr. E. D. Nixon, the parsonage where Dr. King lived, and at two black Montgomery churches. Violent, mean-spirited people also threatened the two white Montgomery judges who had ruled—on the lawsuit filed by attorney Fred Gray—that segregated bus seating was unconstitutional.

It was only by luck and the grace of God that no one was killed in the bombings. Dr. King's home was actually bombed twice. On the first occasion, he was preaching at an evening meeting, and his wife, Coretta, and their infant child, Yolanda, were at the parsonage with a friend, Mrs. Roscoe Williams. Fortunately, they were in the back of the house when the bomb exploded.

Dr. King was quickly summoned from the church, and by the time he arrived home, a large crowd of blacks had gathered outside. They were angry about this cowardly attack, and many in the crowd were calling loudly for revenge. The situation was ugly, and the white law enforcement officers who had arrived were fearful of the crowd's anger.

But when Dr. King arrived, after comforting his wife and child, he spoke to the crowd, reminding them that violence was no answer to violence, and asking them to give the law enforcement officers a chance to do their jobs. In the face of Dr. King's courage and dedication to non-violence, the crowd calmed and went home.

Several white men were arrested for the bombing of the parsonage, but they were not convicted. In fact, no white person was ever convicted for the violent acts committed during the bus boycott period.

But the boycott went on. For 382 days, the buses in Montgomery remained mostly empty. Meanwhile, the court cases made their way through the state and federal courts and all the way to the United States Supreme Court. Finally, the Supreme Court unanimously upheld the decision by Montgomery Judges Frank M. Johnson, Jr., and Richard T. Rives that segregated bus seating was unconstitutional. The Montgomery officials could delay no longer, and they had to allow blacks and whites to sit anywhere they wanted.

With this victory, the Montgomery Bus Boycott was finally over. An important battle for the civil rights of African Americans had been won.

In the years to come, Dr. Martin Luther King, Jr., would go on to even greater recognition as a national and international leader before he was tragically murdered by an assassin in 1968.

Mrs. Parks, however, had become such a symbol of the boycott that it was hard for her or her husband to get a job in Montgomery. So they moved to Detroit, Michigan, where Mrs. Parks worked in the office of a United States congressman.

Mr. Nixon, Mrs. Carr, attorney Gray, and other leaders of the boycott stayed in Montgomery and continued to work to end racial discrimination. Even though the bus seating was no longer segregated, almost every other aspect of life in Montgomery remained racially divided.

One of the most important areas that needed attention was the schools. Although the Supreme Court had ruled in 1954 that segregated education violated the rights of African Americans, the schools in Montgomery—and throughout the South—were still separate.

Although there were many dedicated black teachers and principals, black schools were underfunded and not as well-staffed and equipped as white schools. For example, when white schools got new textbooks, their used, out-of-date books were often "handed-down" to black schools. Also, African American students were offered fewer advanced classes which were necessary to prepare them for college classes that would lead to professional careers.

Attorney Fred Gray wanted to bring a lawsuit against the segregated Montgomery schools, but he needed a qualified plaintiff. Arlam and John-nie Carr discussed this with their son, Arlam Jr., who agreed to be the test applicant to the white schools.

The lawsuit was filed, and Judge Frank John-son, Jr., ruled that the Montgomery school segregation also violated the United States Constitution.

Over the years, Mrs. Carr and her family worked hard in the Montgomery community. Arlam Jr. graduated from the previously all-white high school in Montgomery, went to college, and got a job in the news department of a local television station.

Change gradually came to Montgomery. Mr. and Mrs. Carr and countless other black citizens took part in voter registration campaigns. As the number of black voters increased, the actions of white politicians began to be less hostile to blacks. Eventually, African Americans were

In 1985, thirty years after her arrest, Mrs. Parks, front, took a commemorative ride with Mrs. Carr on a Montgomery bus

elected to the city and county governments, to the school board, and to other important positions in Montgomery. Other changes in employment laws and the attitudes of white employers led to more equal job opportunities.

Although racial discrimination was still a big problem in the United States, Mrs. Carr and Mrs. Parks could look back over the seven decades that they had known each other and be proud of the advancements that they helped to bring to their city, state, and nation.

B y the year 2000, as the world celebrated a new century, Arlam and Johnnie Carr had been retired from the insurance business for many years. But they never retired from community life.

Since 1968, Mrs. Carr has been the president of the Montgomery Improvement Association, the organization once led by her friend Dr. Martin Luther King, Jr. The Carrs were active in their church, in local charities, and in the organization that holds an annual Emancipation Day commemoration service in Montgomery.

Mr. and Mrs. Carr worked every election day as polling officials. In recent years they were active in organizations like One Montgomery, the Friendly Supper Club, and Leadership Montgomery. These organizations seek to bring black and white citizens together for the common goals that all people of good will share—decent homes,

Being awarded an honorary doctorate degree

good jobs, proper educations, and a future for their children that is free of fear and hate.

The year 2005 was a sad one for Mrs. Carr. Her beloved husband of 61 years died after a brief illness and was laid to rest in Montgomery. And then, just a few weeks before the world was going to observe the 50th anniversary of the Montgomery Bus Boycott, her childhood friend, Rosa Parks, died. Mrs. Carr grieved for her husband and her friend, but she also celebrated their long, rich lives and gave thanks to God that she had shared so much with them.

For the next two years, Mrs. Carr remained in remarkably good health. She continued to live in the modest house—the one with the historic marker in front commemorating her and Mr. Carr's roles in the civil rights movement—on Hall Street in Montgomery, next door to her church, the Hall Street Baptist Church. Sometimes she still drove herself to meetings and appointments. She continued to give inspiring speeches to tour groups and students and was an honored dignitary at events like the inauguration of Alabama's governor.

And every day when the weather permitted, during the growing season, Mrs. Johnnie Carr tended the little garden that was right outside her back door. The tomatoes, okra, peas, and beans she grew there reminded her of her childhood "in the rural" outside Montgomery. And the cycle of life that they represented also reminded her that there is a greater good, if we open our hearts to it.

And then, on February 22, 2008, when she was 97 years old, Mrs. Carr passed gently away after suffering a stroke. Her funeral was attended by hundreds of family, friends, and admirers from across the nation.

The End

Terms to Understand

assassin — a murderer who attacks by ambush or surprise.

bail — money paid to get a person out of jail.

bond — an agreement to do something, backed up by money or property that is lost if the agreement is not kept.

boycott — a protest in which people refuse to buy, use, or sell items or a service.

bigotry — blind belief in ideals.

commemorative — celebrating an event or occasion.

custody — control over another person's whereabouts.

discrimination — when one group is treated unfairly compared to another.

Emancipation Day — an observance commemorating the date on which President Abraham Lincoln freed the slaves.

industrial school — one preparing students for crafts and trades.

Ku Klux Klan — a secret, violent white supremacist group.

oppression — keeping someone or some group down.

orator — a person who talks well in public.

ordinance — a regulation or law.

plaintiff — the person filing a legal action in court.

polling — counting, especially of votes in elections.

pneumonia — a disease affecting a victim's lungs.

porter — an attendant who helps passengers with their bags and other needs.

Pullman car — a railroad car with a compartment for sleeping.

racism — a belief that one racial group is inferior to another.

scuppernong — a type of grape often grown in the South.

segregation — keeping one group apart from another.

spinster — an old-fashioned term for a woman who has never married.

sweet milk — a Southern term for plain milk, as opposed to buttermilk.

"The Three R's" — an expression referring to early education which emphasized reading, "'riting," and "'rithmetic."

tyranny — harsh, cruel, and unjust use of authority.

unconstitutional — in violation of the United States Constitution.

wages — pay received for a job.

white supremacy — a philosophy that members of the white race are superior to any others

Index